W0081455

JAMIE HOOD

HOW TO BE A GOOD GIRL

Jamie Hood is a critic, memoirist, poet, and the author of *how to be a good girl*, one of *Vogue*'s Best Books of 2020, *Trauma Plot,* and *regards, marcel*, a monthly newsletter on Proust and other miscellany. Her work has appeared in *The Baffler, Bookforum, The Nation, Los Angeles Review of Books, The New Inquiry, The Drift*, and elsewhere. She lives in Brooklyn.

ALSO BY JAMIE HOOD

Trauma Plot: A Life

HOW TO BE A GOOD GIRL

HOW TO BE A GOOD GIRL

A MISCELLANY

JAMIE HOOD

VINTAGE BOOKS
A Division of Penguin Random House LLC
New York

FIRST VINTAGE BOOKS EDITION 2025

Copyright © 2020 by Jamie Hood

Penguin Random House values and supports copyright. Copyright fuels
creativity, encourages diverse voices, promotes free speech, and creates a vibrant
culture. Thank you for buying an authorized edition of this book and for complying
with copyright laws by not reproducing, scanning, or distributing any part of it in any
form without permission. You are supporting writers and allowing Penguin Random
House to continue to publish books for every reader. Please note that no part
of this book may be used or reproduced in any manner for the purpose of
training artificial intelligence technologies or systems.

Published by Vintage Books, a division of Penguin Random House LLC,
1745 Broadway, New York, NY 10019. Originally published in
paperback in the United States by Grieveland, in 2020.

Vintage and colophon are registered trademarks of Penguin Random House LLC.

Cataloging-in-Publication Data is available at the Library of Congress.

Vintage Books Trade Paperback ISBN: 979-82-17-00684-7
eBook ISBN: 979-82-17-00685-4

Book design by Angelo Maneage

penguinrandomhouse.com | vintagebooks.com

Printed in the United States of America
1st Printing

The authorized representative in the EU for product safety and
compliance is Penguin Random House Ireland, Morrison Chambers,
32 Nassau Street, Dublin DO2 YH68, Ireland, https://eu-contact.penguin.ie.

*for mom, in love & gratitude for
which no words suffice*

*& for Olive, my little dear,
my best girl, who anchored &
adored me in my greatest grief*

[how one moment touches on another moment and a thought flickers on and off]

C.D. WRIGHT
SHALLCROSS

CONTENTS

I.

an

achronology

the

diaries

...

Is "I" even me or am "I"
a gearshift to get from one
sentence to the next?

CLAUDIA RANKINE
DON'T LET ME BE LONELY

[tues mar 24]

i stretch beneath a sugar maple   sweaty   sated

jacket crumpled under ass   sun warming skin

two or three weeks further in to the season the tree will flower

w its yellowish-green small blooms   gathering

& hugging in clusters at the tail of the stalk—

what is called the *pedicel*—& the clusters   the stalk's
                          wondrous

             inflorescences

some sprouting thing wilds its limbs in me!

there is the dream of spring   readying its loveliness ;
                          then

its certain smell   wet woodiness   life

infiltrating the nostrils   its quality of damp
               sex   awakening

i feel i am foaling or ;   i fear i am

foaling   some new project all wily

coalesces in me ; here i lie   in *the last forest*

in brooklyn   joyous; harboring numberless lives

which yawn   open & chirp   the sun laps at us each & all

we are in the thick of a day   alive & newly born

i go to wikipedia; find

the land here at prospect park is the result of a moraine marking off the ter-
minus of the wisconsin glacier, which so formed its *accumulation of uncon-
solidated glacial debris* some 17,000 years past; once forested & bogged &
driven, eventually, to open pasture, by 200 years of european colonization—
the forests having predominantly inspired fear in the colonists & (i read in
alison cobb's *green-wood*) w one such explorer in charge of "indian removal,"
lewis cass, remarking the "indian" is *perhaps destined to disappear w the forest*

there is no story of this country not founded in forcible vanishings

i think *fuck cass*   his willfully passive invocations of *destiny*   motiveless
disappearance

as though an incidental happening in the inexorable & indeliberate hand of
god   no ;

such erasures;   seizures   of land

                    institutions of private property
                                        annihilation

                                              of native peoples; flora; fauna

a violent production   of landscapes   then
falsely mythologized   as *naturally occurring*
                                        same as poetry
                    this fiction   of the oracularity of
                              such births   as

                    poets may proffer

shall the poem delete its own production   & where
                    ghastly traces dew & linger

my gut usage of birth metaphors here; that subliminal concession to literary
traditions of coding woman's art-making as biological; inadvertent;
unconscious—

                    as in the pythia;

                              o   some god speaks through me

think of plath referring to edith sitwell & marianne moore as *aging giant-esses* of the literary world; think also of the term *poetess*, itself a delimita-tion apart from the wor(l)d of the (male) Poet; an insult; this designation

                              in difference to

plath, in the journals, however—naming herself *arrogant*;
naming herself *The Poetess of America*

              or; what demand on a poesis divorced from the
                              tactile taint of its necessary labor

                        keats' belief that a *poem needs*

          understanding through the senses

                                        it is an experience beyond

                    thought poetry soothes &

emboldens the soul to accept the mystery

                  (a preoccupying biographical inquiry on keats:

did he die a virgin & oh! how sad)

the poet-as-mystic: dividing form from its contexts; the invisibilized priv-ilege of the Romantic, the *flaneur*, the meditative wanderer—whose labor facilitates such lackadaisical acceptances of mystery; & these roles, too, feminized, although presumed male

(keats' sense, in tradition w the Romantics, of femaleness as coextensive w death; woman made reducible to the body; or, woman as symbology; the mortal form in decay)

cobb reminds us that *plato banned poetry from his ideal city bc it might arouse dangerous emotions [...] like a woman, such imagery might seduce men into unleashing their own feelings; they might lose control over* the city within

                                        for whom is *self-*
          reliance even possible   i intermix my literary
                                        traditions & do
                                        not care

my *city within* is a confetti of possible thought-housings; & is in despair

*

{NOTE: tues aug 25: consider the last six months & that my writing this
book has only been made materially possible by a commingling of crises;
the anxious swaths of the pandemic's out-of-time time; the redirection
of my self-documentary impulse in a moment we have been denied the
capacity to narrate ourselves in our usual social contexts; a need—not to
produce an aesthetic object *as such*—but, as is always my artistic imperative—
to make new worlds from all this pain, this cavernous desire, this collective
fear; which is, finally, perhaps only a more circuitous variation on a
contemporary obsession w productivity-for-its-own-sake

ofc also the fact that i ~~was fortunate enough to receive~~ have been on un-
employment insurance}

*

[return here to tues mar 24]

i am turned on by process: its baldness, the laborious configuration of
clustering thoughts—inflorescences—into a story for all to see; to be
stretched; perceived

~~think suddenly, inexplicably, of a catherine wheel—the exposure of the
art-object's innards—to be flayed for the *peanut crunching crowd*—twirling
& widening in rhythm w their need~~

~~but why this metaphor?~~ i am in joy in my writing, although it at times is
torturous

i love it in its labyrinthine & infuriating mechanics & stops & starts & the
messinesses

on twitter ~~i feel~~ i often see writers who love the opposite—to make a show
of despising the work of it & i acknowledge them ~~although they are not my
kin~~

i wonder if the performative disavowal of the *process* of art—that hoisting
up of the *i hate writing* flag—largely invests its energy in marking the
art-object itself as a pseudo-spiritual ineluctability—the thing which had
to manifest through the body of the artist-as-conduit; in other words,

a redirection here of an old trope: the *anti-capitalist*-poet-as-mystic, the
one who acknowledges the fact of the labor & cannot be thought to be
fetishizing it

oppositely, do i fetishize the labor of it to insist on my being taken seriously

(i am not taken seriously)

i am fascinated by the process, my contexts, have this insufferable need to
draw the steely world into which i have been born & to which i am

                                in turn accountable

to exhibit what some god hath wrought; what has brought me—still—
here;

        here;   here:

                lying

quietened   & cautious   examining

        bee balm; little bluestem;   &

                        birds   who flit

                        about me

species which nest here:

the green heron   w its ungainly flight; its low gulping song—but shrill
signal—decidedly echoing; sounds of
                                                    wetlands

the wood duck   a close relative of the celebrity central park
mandarin; among the most beautiful of the waterfowl; the females w their
                                                    distinctive &   delicate
                        white feather patterns about the eyes

the severe visage of the brown thrasher, foraging in its
                                tangled thickets   piercing skin & membranes
                        of dogs or people who venture too near their nests

the yellow warblers   bright & gentle   sometimes
        so small as to be tangled
                in an orb-weaver's web   ;
                that unmistakable call
                sweet sweet sweet   *i'm so sweet*

the orchard oriole   migrating south soonest in summer

also (in the last decade) the red-tailed hawk

et cetera   & i think

how the sugar maple under which i lie will, around the fourth of july, begin
to lose its green vibrancy, to brown & fade   & still   i think

what luck   to exist   to write at all   to write

some new thing   at the edge of the world

& in company of more life

                                    *

i ramble

in '67 that *aging giantess* marianne moore takes up the cause of prospect
park's gnarled *camperdown elm* & immortalizes the behemoth in a poem,
calls the tree *our crowning curio*—the elm a gift from one mr. a. burgess in
1872; one of the first of its kind in the country

it is still leafing; / still there. / mortal though (moore)

{a poem of great delight in life   its singularity & pleasure in
spite—perhaps in fact *because of*

        —inevitable decline

     we too! mortal though

& again i think of plath—having facilitated the cessation of her own life
some four years earlier—in the coldest london winter in a century—away
from the countryside home where her marriage had dissolved—& where
there stood a yew tree which; likewise; she rendered eternal in a poem

      yet;

        in plath's yew tree   no joy of life
                   rather   ;
                   an edifice
           to epistemological & existential collapse
        meaninglessness   *the message* [...]
         is blackness—

           blackness and silence}

i should like a project which

wields such systems of roots   who anchor

& hide   i should   like one thousand thousand branching
motions

i should like passage of invisible air systems through a theme
that wind-dance

disaffiliating each from each

i should like to loosen the rapt ribbon of my tongue

let it unravel as the world does

     to show its hand

     imbibe chaos of presence & open

i should like the project to be a mess as i am a mess

poetry   fragments   repurposed diary entries   other shit

shit   traceable—as *schism* & *schizo* are—to the proto-indo-european *skei*

to cast off   *to cut*   & *split*

i should like to shear (from *sker*) artifice

to facilitate & incorporate the indeterminate

umbilicus between *process draft   poem   art-function*

i don't know if the miscellany will orient   become
                                              some object

but i feel a thrill of purpose

i feel an unfurling

tucked away from the maw of the world, the body's aching hums more insistently; i attend to the rhythm of its needs in ways which are not materially or temporally possible for me while bartending five or six nights per week

i am eating well, sleeping regularly (although the sleep itself, more frustratingly interrupted than even it usually is w my nightmares—this inchoate anxiety!), drinking hardly at all; also, i've quit smoking, this time i think for good; think, thank god

today i am wondering if i will ever be well-fucked again

think of G   who has gone away   how glad i was

freed of his condescension   sad also; missing his delight

(the sex   however   tepid;

him too tentative & his frame   frail his smallness
                                     darling in its way—

          i felt   while riding him   like some Godzilla

imagined pedestrians fleeing a city block   imagined

          accidentally crushing him   in my great force!
                                         later laughed...)

                              *

mom calls to wish me a happy birthday

the virus worsening in her city   & ofc decimating ours

ask self now   *will we meet again*

in relation to every one i love   on the phone

keep my   self   from weeping

knowing it will only upset us both further

cry instead once the call has ended

olive curling nearer me   her furrowed brow

her warmth—my little oven—her human worrying

i knead her furry haunches & console her

console my self too   ; god;   half-hearted

                                    *

although not especially *into* G

ask what had been wrong w me

that he would trail off ;   blame my

self   for the fizzling   even though

i had no desire

          to pursue any joined future

i have convinced myself each relationship failure is a failure on the level of
my personhood

not *what did we do* but   *why am i unlovable*   that is;
              why am i   i

& know this is abusive self-talk

trauma speaking through me to me—its virus-like quality; preoccupied in
self-   replication at the potentially fatal expense of its host

          viruses as *organisms at the edge of life*

                              sapping life   lapping

              at its juices

starved of it as we all shall one day be starved

trauma like silt compounding   en/soiling   its   self

across   time

trauma of time's passing—a sensibility i cannot fathom w/o considering
woolf & her lighthouse & how

*nothing, it seemed, could survive the flood, the profusion of darkness which,
creeping in at keyholes and crevices, stole round window blinds, came into
bedrooms, swallowed up here a jug and basin, there a bowl of red and yellow
dahlias, there the sharp edges and firm bulk of a chest of drawers. not only
was furniture confounded; there was scarcely anything left of body or mind by
which one could say, "this is he" or "this is she" [...] somebody laughed aloud as
if sharing a joke w nothingness*

trauma   an obsidian eye   which

regards the being in which it secures its home

w true indifference   we;

passes to be steered through

*

i should like to know what sufferance

is demanded   i would like to be a good girl

or; to ascertain whether such metaphysical category

as such exists   & is it stable   or; am

i

i am writing toward a being

or;   away from my undone

-ness   each project

a configuration of a me

in utterable tapestries

i wish to produce

a self   so as to acquire one

even if such ontology secures its

beingness only in the moment of its emittance

the blinking out of a star in its death rattles

a gas lamp snuffed in the wind of a sudden pressure

system   then the overwhelming clear—

when i was a girl a sphere of diaphanous light

appeared at the front window & clotted

about its self in our living room

an electrical phenomenon known

plainly   as *ball lightning*

rare   accompanied at times

by an acrid odor   a low hissing

               anything may seem to have been an act of god

if u are filled w enough need

as i am

i would value nothing so greatly as the certainty of my goodness

i do not mean to indicate a sort of nicety

nor   perhaps   even kindness

is my seeking merely   evaluative   a longing
        for an appraisal

~~i see the subject of course as a~~ what is this calcification   of ~~minute experiences~~ experience   transmogrifying inside
time

                a what congealing

~~(thus   our foundational instabilities)~~

~~(thus   the ineluctable opacity of the other to the self / the self to its own occupant)~~

~~(thus~~   {the great precarity transposition
                                in language)}

to what extent is my need to be imagined as good merely a proof that more
of my self is bound up in the attention of & legitimation by others than is
usual   or useful

butler: *the 'I' first comes into being as a 'me' through being acted upon by an Other*

if i were to lose sight of this pearl   this perceptibility
would i cease in a becoming

is the *i* which i write an Other   is the writerly-subject

                ; that is

is the *i-which-writes* an Other   a self   or;
          is there an inescapable severance

if i am present in a subject position what responsibility do i have to the content, to the truth value, of the words themselves (rankine)

          are we founded on fracture

is the discontinuity the single continuous thread

[§§§]

before fleeing did ariadne ask the minotaur if he understood her to be what one might call a *person*

or; should she cease in the being of one beyond the borders of the labyrinth

[weds jul 15]

do i render my   self   Other   to my   self
in the purgative event of the utterance

[fri jul 17]

purge   from the latin *purgare*   to purify

at the outset of quarantine my doctor & i

adjust my estrogen dosage

& i spend a week kneeling over the toilet

each morning   {holy; holy} & crying

all afternoon   crying for the metaphorical

            proximity

of this experience —this morning sickness which has

            plagued

      me in each event

of hormonal adjustment—   to a pregnancy

                  i will never have

            bad girl

i think of nothing but puke for weeks

having been apparently so full of it

& so hollowed out in this talismanic

emptying

in grad school my puking   {paired w frantic exercise;
                            fasting; et cetera}

          another sort of a ritual

          a contemplated process

          a thoughtfulness

i learn to configure my own smallness

to render the body

          a managed thing

          little corn-husk doll   flailing its thin arms
                          pins through   her its eyes

          recall lying face-flat on cobblestone

          limbs akimbo   boston;   a hell

          i institute the frailty of the good girl

          as is anything the body   is a deliberation

          it passes through many hands

          is inscribable

          & has at times its kind of speech

                                *

i do not associate the onset of my ED w the series of three [redacted]
events in the third year of my doctorate

these three [redacted] events did not, in any conscious sense i would let
my/self register, transpire

the morning after the first of these i tell my roommate; i tell my best
friend; i pale beneath their blank eyes; & say nothing more

for some years i run nine to 15 miles four times/week; my average pace hovers around a six-&-a-half minute mile; my sprint speedier

i drop weight; approach my pubertal thinness of around 110lbs, although i am now nearly six feet tall

at this time i am living in somerville; on these runs i cry in nearly every possible bend around the charles

there are memories i have fashioned into survivable past-tenses only inasmuch as i have divested my/self from the thing that i seem to have been—this *thing* which may, in some remarkable moments, appear to present-me to have cohered

i think—~~in perhaps a too-easy associational move~~—of louise bourgeois' *spider* (1996); of the quite real bones hollowed of their marrow; resting in the spider's steel cage; between its bronze legs *en pointe*

my mother was a tapestry woman (bourgeois)

bourgeois' intensity of attention to the *re/creative* potentiality of returning to the past; to childhood; to old trauma

in *I REDO* (1999–2000), the woman seated on the tapestried chair under the bell jar; the infant rising up above her like a balloon, attached still by the umbilicus; the claustrophobic capacity of what we have left behind; & what we are yet anchored to

i place my palm over my tummy   ask

        what is held here

it is astonishing how separable the mind may be from the body when the body in which u live is not a body the world believes should subsist

in mad men, don telling peggy *this never happened; it will shock u how much it never happened*

the body is dumb   *the body is meat* (anne sexton)

my ED one more cliché in the bucket of what someone on twitter mockingly refers to as my "laundry list of personal traumas" *only the summer was sweet* (sexton)

every day i wake up & wish i would stop telling on my/self

& go on doing it

does each formulation of the feminine   or;   each trans-
gression of it require a sacrifice of the flesh; fresh bodies for the cultural
meat grinder

the tv movie *perfect body* (1997) starring amy jo johnson as a gymnast
struggling w bulimia

which we watched in junior high   & which i felt near to

having done gymnastics my   self   having grown too tall
to continue competitively

my body   imperfect   going broader   o

to be teen-aged; a horror! in that all puberty is monstrous

that first stark encounter w the physical disturbances of aging

                                        grotesquerie

i remember quite clearly in the movie the moment the mother discovers
the jars of vomit amy jo johnson's character secrets away in her closet

            a revelation of the troublesome

                        spillage of womanform

the mrs bates moment   a terror of taxidermy
            retention of expunged materiality

what is sloughed off—   physical waste   ;

            philosophically speaking

            a kristevan encounter w the abject   a disturbance   of *identity*
as   such   the subject facing   its *already-deadness*

i google *puke* & see its first recorded usage found in shakespeare's famous
"seven ages of man" speech from *as u like it*

but—

i lose interest

or; else grow distracted

in undirected weeping

another purgation

tears are like smiles   in that they can be true or false
but they are also worse   than smiles
bc they can mean absolutely nothing (james elkin)

the uncontrollable crying of margery kempe

a mystic's body wracked in pleasure

& pain   doubts sprung up   in bystanders;
had they been witness to the power of christ
manifest in the material world

or;

to just another hysterical showboat

or;

statues of the virgin mother weeping her tears of blood

or;

crying as spiritual affect—to weep in the presence of art or history; a kind
of entanglement w divinity which can overwhelm the eye   ;

obliterate   the   *i*

it is increasingly uncertain to me whether we have even the most minute
force of control over the expressibilities of the body

all my attempts at managing mine having changed little to nothing about
the orchestration of my body by a world which marks it as communally
perceptible

that is;

the endless cultural articulabilities

of the form i hang my "person" on

which i am   finally

powerless before

[sat apr 11]

if i were to stop time   what would i have   been

in isolation i feel high all the time

indeed as if time has ceased to pass

a day could be a week or a month   40 seconds

i am thinking of the burial trenches in hart park

i am thinking of the publicity of this collective grief

      its disorienting spectacle

i am thinking of desubjectivization as it coagulates

      on an axis wherein the body is an erotic fixture & also a frailty—
subject to its eventual & necessary
         termination

this terminus suddenly so proximate; suddenly as near
        as a tongue on the nipple or the lobe of the ear

     where if i am bitten   licked ;
        my eyes   rollback;   mouth/parts

the involuntarism of certain iterations of pleasure

i am thinking i need to be touched

     & that it is more illegal than it has ever been

in isolation i am perceived by men hardly at all

which is to say   am i discernible in the first instance

in the context of my girlness   that friction ;

                    oppositional / gendering   energies

my need for a good fuck to elaborate my personhood

there is no man to tell me if i am good or not

there never has been

or;

is the subject—having been in some way previously constituted in an inter-
subjective context—when apart from the *other*

            even   gendered / even   sexed

i touch my   self to find out

i fuck my   self to find out

& there are no answers

[thurs aug 20]

i am always writing toward a positionality

a lookout tower   in which i might operate

    as a center

i've rewritten this manuscript 13 times in six months & still cannot decide
on its start

in grad school a mentor laughs   *it's turtles all the way down*

me going   *huh*

          *

i adore drafts

i am a perfectionist obsessed w the incomplete

i feel the only writers i have felt in intimacy w lately are those who are
endlessly citational; who show their work

who integrate the anxiety of this sort of a birth {that metaphor again} into
their writerly-*i*

i would watch words set off like mist in their synapses & course downward
through the nerves   veins   viscera   & blood-jet
          of the body until—

arriving in the fingers

being pounded into the tap tap tap of their little keyboards

if i could

i keep everything about my self

& work   entirely private

until i shuck the casing &

offer all of me up like a still-warm heart

to the wicked queen of TOTAL PUBLICITY

when i am exposed to the world i no longer have any care at all

eat me   *drink me*   i am disinterested in opacity

i do not know how to be

i desire instruction & so write [it out] for my/self

& fail /

to instruct

how to be a good girl

chin down   eyes up   digital fantasia likes to fuck

a mouth blooms   (a wet spot spreads over the sheets
                       illicit)

& widens   accepts two fingers

two lingerings   two depressors   what dark duet

gag   ;   no   don't gag

                                 o

uvular stopgap   of the feminine

re   cognize   u are

a facilitation   a sorrow

        between solids

        even god was an embryo before time

        keep records

& begin again

how to be a good girl

when u have reached the gape
pit of the world   ask
a man what he wants u to do
& do it

this is the molten core around which
a civilization accretes   this is a horror
in a sea cave   the pre-lapsarian howl
this is a need   then   a duty
lap at the stone foot   & quiet

                        now

begin again

how to be a good girl

pluck   nothing   from the vine

                                    & eat of it

behold   ;   a universe unbraids its
                                    cascade of lovely hairs

if He shall name it

u are to be fucked by it   all spectacularity

all eyed   all mirrored   o goodness

speak   &   undoings fall from ur plump open

cough   &   death seeks the hiddens of ur tooths

shriek   &   there shall be a plundering of stars

or do nothing

& be as much

beg   in

          again

good girl

                                    *

he says   yes   good

girl   spanking me

across his knee   palm opened

wide as the pupils of god are wide

i am his good girl   & i

reside in the *thwack* of his hand

he knows & he says he knows

i hide what i want   still

i pride my   self   in the pleasures i earn

thwack   this punishment

of the bad girl—as though

reversed   a card pulled

as from a taroc pack

my tits press against his thighs   o

nipples ache w the slack disorder

of the world   his pressure   *thwack*

stuffing me up into me   bear baptism

concealing my lack   this cover of indeterminacy

i kneel upon adjacencies of meaning

i concede control to fantasy

~~the oracle requests a folded towel~~

even in supplication   i am choosy   *thwack*

                   when allowed

          & i am panting

enough to confess there are some numbered lilac days

who slide inside me   & hang here

overripely stone-fruiting & times

where what i need more than satisfaction is   *thwack*

          a relief of prostration

as when i   longing   lie

back beneath the hand of a man

this slakes   the undoings at my center

who knows such grim thirst in heaven

i am dusking   i cicada

a trumpeting of cherubs

winged & deathly &

then   hush

the world in the dulled throb of need

my ass pinks & begs

my slick mouth begs   it whimpers

my opening whimpers under him

o lord   i am widening   & i am

open & i am open & i am open & i

am open i am open i am

the pupil of god & it is god

who knows what i am become

[??? aug ??]

the above is the first poem i write for this project: a lament for my failed relationship of last spring—one of the three i allude to in the housewife essay i publish w *the new inquiry* in february of this year

i want to serve, i need to serve. i live for serving or i feel worthless (bourgeois)

that ex; so talented in dispensing spankings, so at ease in taking control of my body when i most needed it, & so careless in anything else having to do w my personhood; my feeling; or;

maybe it is that i asked too much

maybe it is always that i ask for something men don't wish to give me

that is;   love

~~i worry over the ethics of writing of him~~

~~but he is anonymized; only he & i know who he is—was; to me~~

~~he'd certainly ensured that our lives never really overlapped~~

~~i was not his secret~~

~~but nor was i a part of his dailiness~~

i was his bad girl his bedroom girl

when i cried that last time

i'd asked if i was just a cumrag   & what had i done

to deserve it

& in that moment he held me in my sobbing & gave no answer

in any case he doesn't read my work; indeed, refused to: i suppose found me trashy or embarrassing in some foundational way

of course i'd thought   he'd come around   ~~some how~~
     ~~some day~~

i write in my diary of last year that i imagined we were in some sort of
an intimacy cold war; that we were on the *long route to him loving me* &
perhaps

were i to wait him out {*be patient*}   i would be made true in his loving
image

& perhaps   i was delusional

& perhaps i gave him credit where no credit was due

& perhaps

       grieved not for him but for foolishness

& perhaps

every instantiation of love is a precursor to mourning

but did i love him or did i want only that he would love me

[fri aug 28]

there are times i find it easier   ;

less emotionally poisonous   ; less   physically grueling

to take men's money than to take their lies

if i were a gold-digger

i should think   i'd have a pocketful of gold

yet here i grasp   at nothing

breadcrumbs in violent woods

i scrape wet sticks   against one another's wet   & pray
                           for fire

the good girl should not talk about money   commodities
      she *is* commodity—a fetish
      in its fleshiest & most perfectible form

i am trying to unlearn my body in its variation as a use-value
unlearn my   self

      as a disposability

i should like to be fathomed

as a/live & know this is quite a lot to ask

although i find my   self   in increasing dis/ease w *preliminary materials for a theory of the young girl* as i interrogate it for dialogue w this project   moments still erupt in the brain

often, before her decay becomes too obvious, the Young-Girl gets married
(tiqqun)

so i apply serums creams   pray my body sustains
          in smoothness for a little while yet

i will my self to be a stilled pool

i will the body towards love   or; something like

i imagine olive in a flower crown   bouquet in her mouth
          my little flower girl   my good girl

i imagine a good man joining himself to me before a god i do not believe in & people i sometimes do i will never be wed

i am a fetish

men;   they pick at my body as vultures on carrion   & toss me once i have
fulfilled my carnal function   rather;   after it has been fulfilled

          in & on me

there are times i have on a technical level agreed to this

then also there are the other times

{i tell my   self   this is not *that* book}

i have been locatable on an itemized bucket list of women to be fucked &
done away w

a fucket list

bad girl

see me?

i have no skills excepting that i am able to be filled by cock & cum

i hope this is valuable at the end of the world

i would barter any   thing   to feel everything

i suspect the angels spy as i rub lotion into my tits
                          they ache

if i could afford therapy perhaps i would tell a professional the things i am
telling u

if i could afford therapy i should be perfectible; a good girl

as far as i am able to tell therapy is a tedious arranging of the self as w an
appointment book

if i schedule my being   pencil my   self in
          i will finally be allowed to rest

treating one's self as an other. supervising oneself (sontag)

i have imagined at times living beyond trauma

then i wake up lol

one day i dream of having health insurance

which is dreaming big   to me

i should like to learn what it is to go to a doctor

i think i could be good at having more strangers' hands on me

i could wear a wedding dress to the office

marry my   self to health   which is a commodity like anything
else   if i owned it i could be more good

                    gooder

if someone could j fix my personhood maybe i could live

i love to fetishize self-improvement

i love even more the wish that a man would manage me
 improve me

it must be such a dream to be a doll

i imagine my grief like a stone pit at my center   a baby

my grief baby is the only baby i shall ever feel kicking inside of me

when i was a girl i dreamed of raising two daughters—two visions, as my
mom had—& to let them be whatever sorts of girls—or otherwise—they
should like to—as my mom did

in the brief breeze the wren ruffles its feathers, shakes, cocks its head
toward me

now i dream of nothing

this is a lie   i night/mare every day

once a client told me he hoped his daughter *never had to do this*—the thing
that i was doing—which, at that precise moment, was cleaning his cum off
my stomach

i like the feel of fitting an envelope of cash into my purse! i like to pretend
i am an extravagance: a joy of waking early to watch blushing peaches &
gauzy pinks streak the whole godish horizon at sunrise; a velvet feeling of
dark chocolate melting in ur mouth after a lover has set it daintily on ur
tongue; the texture of my curls after they have air-dried in sea-wind; or
love

rather than whatever it is i have been

if i were better positioned perhaps i would have told my client that, in the
first instance, any girl whose father could afford to easily pay my rate was
probably set for life; & that, in the second instance, i also hoped she never
had to clean his cum off her stomach

although this is what some daughters have withstood

if i had two daughters i too might hope they would elude the life i have
had to survive

it feels less risky to transcribe my worst thoughts, as i am doing, knowing i shall never have daughters who will wrestle the consequences of reckoning w them

not subjecting my theoretical daughters to my life is, in its way, a relief

i wish many things had been different

& i find regret a useless affect

[sat aug 8]

the television show *good girls* is as i understand it largely about what women resort to bc the world hates us too much to let us be alive

the show stars christina hendricks, retta, and mae whitman as three women who, as it were, *break bad* after "struggling to make ends meet" for some time w/o any survivable transformation

the media adores nothing more than a woman brought low

i am eminently subjectable to hurt   or is it ˉ ;

i am immanently subjectable to hurt

if i get out of bed on any given day i tell my self this is an achievement

i know that having a bed is itself a luxury & has been taken from me before;

could again be at any time

i think if i had christina hendricks' waist a man might want to love rather than destroy me

i think if i had christina hendricks' *mad men* money i could j *buy* a christina hendricks waist

i could reformulate the surfaces of my body

although—

i imagine it costs a pretty penny more to fix the interior

rape has happened to me more often than love & there are days this
appears to me usual;   also boring

i don't want to be raped again   although—i suppose such a
thing has nothing to do w my desire

if i were truly a good girl   shouldn't i be w/o   desire

there is no one in this world who would protect me

bad girl

i bite the inside of my cheek & say (again)   this is not my rape
book this is not my rape book this is not my rape book

every book is my rape book

bad girl bad girl bad   girl bad girl

my rape book is 300 pages long &

i will never finish writing it

the woolf essay i have been working on is stalled out

did woolf kill her   self bc of the war or bc she feared that writing
was through w her

this is another sort of a war   & one whose battles only matter to
the generals

　　　　　or whatever military metaphor makes sense here
　　　　　i don't read books for dads

　　　　　i j suck their dicks & that is my duty

when women artists die we are spoken of as incandescences; lighting at
some unsustainable candlepower

*a destiny of such violent self-definition does not always bring the real person
nearer* (hardwick on plath)

i think i write an awful lot about women artists who killed themselves
considering i am j a bitch whose depression does not manifest in suicidal
ideation

[sun aug 23]

what is the most humiliating fact of ur life

i think mine is i've known the song i'd like as the first at my wedding for the last decade

an old jazz standard

this is my one secret   i can say no more

as i rinsed the conditioner from my hair the other morning it began playing on my speaker & i sat on the floor of the tub & wept

                              shameful

            all this insatiable need

i feel i could burn up in it

perhaps what i mean is i wish it would burn me up already

                         *

i wish at times i could divest my   self

of such sentimentalism   ;   such self-pitying

i am excising what i am able but i am running out of time

every writer has some story about how their book was 50 thousand billion pages & they purged all but 70 & found there a work of genius

i find the notion of *genius* politically detestable

but perhaps this is only a sign that i am not one

[sun aug 16]

if this book doesn't make money i am not sure how to survive the winter

people do not seem to understand the depths to which they will sink for enough cash to live until they have in fact sunk to them

me telling u this doesn't change a lack of perspective & i'm sorry for it

sucking dick for money is simple

begging for money is nearly untenable

                                        but only nearly

i wish i might make art beyond the anxiety of pay; but then i would have to have been a trust fund baby; & probably i would have made no art at all

                                *

could anyone blame me for taking cash when it is dangled before my dumb face

i am not a capitalist

i could wear the *capitalism ruins everything around me* t-shirt & not tell a lie

i want only enough to get by

there are days i think i should like to live a little longer

i know this is a stupid thing

bad girl

[weds apr 22]

is this a book on love

& why should i imagine my   self

having any such ridiculous expertise on the subject

i tell one of the men i had been dating leading up to the pandemic that my affairs w men have been historically inconsistent

& then think of sontag in her journals remarking that in the life of the child consistency is an enemy, *for to be consistent* [...] *is already a limitation on desire*

if i say in love i am a child

it has its kind of beauty

although the inconsistency of my loving has brought nothing but agony

i search the etymology of *agony* & am led to christ's suffering in the garden of gethsemane & rethink my usage of this word

although i was raised outside of religion & have no fear of my heretical speech   ;

for the bad girl—speech is heretical by default

it burbles in my witch-mouth

i incapacitate by my stony gaze

agon from the greek *agonia*

in struggle for victory   *as in wrestling*

one night that man i had been dating leading up to the pandemic puts his
hands around my throat consentlessly & it is more or less over after this

i learn while listening to a podcast that in his defense against charges of
battering his ex-wife nicole brown on new year's day in 1989, oj simpson
suggests perhaps that he had *wrestled* her; a phraseology lead defense
attorney johnnie cochran will later take up during detective john edwards'
testimony in the murder trial, contesting said testimony concerning the
abuse by saying the couple had, if one were to really think on it, probably j
been *engaged in mutual wrestling*

the connectivities between various traumas is fragile

      like muslin

affective textures pool & brush one another

tap-dance in overlapping statics

i aim not to insinuate an indistinguishability here but to inquire what
exactly it is that has happened to me in this life

he was not the first &

some mistakes i can no longer abide

or i tell my   self i will not   & live in hope

that my fortitude of will subsists

                              *

is this a book on love

or its lack   & the fact that its lack

renders me suspect on the level of my goodness

what value does love confer on the subject

i'm asking u a question

—answer me

after the death of his mother, roland barthes writes of his astonishment &
anxiety over this loss as a reckoning w *not a lack* [...] *but a wound, some-
thing that has harmed love's very heart*

& i think there are certain griefs in love we survive

but just barely   which cipher

off the expansiveness of the heart

delimit its possible futurity, its lovings

such griefs defy chronology   as trauma disorganizes time

                    disorients & displaces us

        from the coherency of narrative   ;

        in my rape book i write how the rape event

disorders the subject's capacity to inhabit & elucidate the story of their
aliveness

                in such sense

defacilitates our capacity to imagine our selves

        as living

barthes: *what i find utterly terrifying is mourning's*
          discontinuous *character*

& all my love poems are poems of mourning

                    out of time

          & i think in a way the erotic frisson of my being

spanked   is necessarily inseparable

from a kind of mourning w/in the violences i have been subject to at the
hands of men; for dignities which were wrested from me;

                    a preciousness lost to history

the discontinuity of mourning is not merely a question of time

that is;   when the affect

                    of my mourning may appear

                    unexpected   ;   a sort of flashback

                    in a future tense

                    where such mourning

                    should have been   left in the past

but also—

               in which contexts this mourning

               alongside which feelings   &

               bringing which other pasts w it

               how peopled

mourning not -as-object   but   *-as-texture*

                              *

i would like to know love which does not cleave me in its outset as a future
loss

                              *

house finches in the park hop about my feet

    my small attendants

i have been revising an old poem about a finch i tried to nurse to health
when i was a girl &   which; of course—   died
    also   the shoe box i buried her in

        some things   i;

    remember

trying on my mother's heels & secreting them away in the back of her closet
as if;

    nothing in the world has ever happened

house finches are a recent addition to the eastern part of the country, i
read, & have been offered a warmer welcome than transplants such as the
house sparrow or the starling, the latter an invasive species where i was
from, &, as such, was legal to shoot at

in 1940 a small number of house finches were set off on long island to
breed, having failed as caged birds, "hollywood finches"

the house finch is strictly vegetarian, even when feeding its nestlings, an
unusual phenomenon in birds

a rare bird;   or;

an odd bird (a favorite phrase)

          *

last night A tear-gassed & roughed up by the LAPD

i think how i should be documenting the protests but feel at a loss; feel
insufficient; feel i have writer friends better-placed, more tapped in, w

more organizational history & political acumen than i; that i wouldn't be interested in reading my own work on this moment; remind my self it is important to shut the fuck up at times, to not bear takes on every aspect of this expansive life

then feel ashamed, as though it is true what [redacted] said of me; that i am a good writer but only inasmuch as i am good at writing about my small self

ofc every project completed has relied at some instance on the denial of the possible gestation of one thousand thousand other possible projects; *gestation*

another birth metaphor   who shall be my children

      & into which world do i bring them

~~{my books cannot love me back}~~

who is my audience? i never know; i write for my   self

                ; hope for others

i break & toss my granola bar to the cobblestones blanketing this small enclosure & imagine these birds adoring me; here; where

i am snow white & want for nothing

the glass coffin deferred another day

i fall into a google hole again; end up researching the ronettes—of especial interest, their march 1963 single "good girls," the group's final w colpix records & one which did not chart, no thanks to the label

disappointed w their representation following the release of "good girls," estelle bennett put in a call to phil spector & asked that he reorient their career

later, after the ronettes had gained further success & lead singer ronnie had married spector, he forbade her from recording in the studio or performing w the group any longer, including during the group's shows opening for the beatles in a short 1968 tour

according to ronnie's memoir, *be my baby: how i survived mascara, mini-skirts, & madness*, spector's issues of control escalated into more & more terrifying patterns of abuse, w ronnie, finally, locked up in his 23-room bluebeard mansion—surrounded w barbed wire & guard dogs—& w/o shoes, which spector had confiscated to prevent her fleeing on foot

in the basement spector had erected a gold coffin w a glass top—telling her it was so he could keep an eye on her always; even after death

w the help of her mother, ronnie eventually escaped, in her bare feet, no less

after spector threatened to hire a hit man to kill her, ronnie agreed, in the divorce settlement, to surrender custody of their adopted children & all future record earnings

what is a *beyond* to trauma ; is a *getting over* only ever directional; a side-stepping across time think of the night we fled west virginia; remember it as through a blizzard, although this may be

a mind's trick; all my memories of that time hushed in winter& there, cocooned in the passenger's seat of my mother's ancient VW bug, i struggled to keep awake—i look now on the small six-year-old self huddled that night as though looking upon a perfectly staged tableau—& think how it is that clearer memories tend to coalesce about themselves, calcify into cinema

my tiny mother's energy behind the wheel of the tiny car crackling, frenetic, an electrical ball; i recall directing my own energy toward hers, trying to join it to mine; nodding off; the dangerous curving mountain passes their own kind of lullaby

the sense that i needed to remain conscious for her sake, that we would only get out if i were to sustain the intensity of my energy, my attention

& we did

in writing of my childhood it is crucial i note that most of it is one round
vast blank

an emptied snow globe i shake seeking some comfort which will not coag-
ulate

there is a little person that must have been a me
        —or something as like—   who for a dozen years retained
only the haziest & most erratic of memories

i do not know how much of this is trauma   or; else; how much
more detail i recall after those first 12 years of my life bc i began to keep
diaries

                        in my poems i notice

i often write the phrase *when i was a girl*

& each time think;   whatever it is that i *was*

               {girlness of this *was*}

      will be taken as an axis of dispute

once a semi-stranger told me i could be *v marketable! quite successful!* if i
were to continue this public flaying of my self instead on the basis of my
so-disputed sex

that is; wrote of my transness as tragic; *the failure of having not been born
cis*

—rather than to take as my writerly preoccupation the architectural &
affective

      bizarrities of desire...

          shelters sought in the wake of trauma...

i said *thank u* & ordered another shot

*

is the trans girl good

that is;   is the trans girl   girled

these are not appropriate channels of interrogation   as far as my interest
orients

they pander to audiences who wish to insinuate the illegitimacy of my
person   hood

      this kills me & my kin

            i do not recognize it

    no one   & nothing should

*

i say *when i was a girl* to envelop my self apart from the world

i say *when i was a girl* bc my girlhood was stolen from me—was defiled—
through several complex & deliberate methodologies

i say *when i was a girl* bc i put faith in the power of repetition

       repetition

which   as nikky finney   reminds us

                              is holy

        to incant my girlness   brings me nearer the gods

to me my transness feels circumstantial rather than originary   or;

i *was* a girl   & later i facilitated a language which made this girlness
comprehensible to

        others

              this   i think   may be good

but there is no knowing; no

i may say only that i was

        ;

here &

will not always be so

[thurs aug 27]

re-reading sontag's *reborn* this week seeking structure in my form
         -lessness   re-reading also

                    may sarton

                    barthes

                    zambreno

thinking always of how the diaristic or autofictional or confessional-*i* is
                                   contextualized
              disavowed

there is a vitality & immediacy to sontag's notebooks which i tend to
think elude her larger body of work, which is hawk-eyed, imperious

i feel a kinship w the sontag of the journals—w her self-flagellation; her
intellectual anxiety; her terror at being, in any real sense, sexually *possessed*;
or out of control

this kinship perches alongside my awed regard of her essays, as if from a
distance; a looking at something quite bright—too much so

i am not a list-keeper although i think i should like to be

i imagine sontag calling my work cheap

i imagine sontag calling me cheap

this touches the erotic

i notice in my center part a half dozen stray gray hairs as if in intimacy; i
press them against my lips in prayer

[thurs may 14]

i envision recitation of process

           like a tilting of the head

      turning the great swan neck   to open air

   revelation of the carotid

    o;   is insistence on mess   exposure

       its kind of truth

       -telling   or;   omittance

of accountability

in *flash bang boom* of spectacle

o love

do i allow u my dermis

as i fortress   my further

in the essay i write on my longing

to become a housewife   i indicate

the structuration of such an identity

as a formulation of *being-w/o-self*

a depopulation of identity

-as-such the good girl as evacuate

but of course what i desire

is to be this thing & to be

loved & burble & throb

in the muck of my shame

did [redacted] ever want to make me cum or was i just his fuck doll

or;   was this different than w any of the other of my men   my "exes"

i think no   i think (stupid)

            i am a wandering wound

i look up & try to understand dark matter   but it all just seems like more matter to me

remember. my ignorance is NOT charming (sontag)

what is the opposite of a something that still somehow manifests; a not-nothing which is also a nothing

plath's endless mirrors & negations in the *ariel* poems

i am always parroting voices   a good girl is a sieve
                                or; i am

      a conduit & not a person

or;   is this merely a way of eliding presentness

or;   is   imagining my self   as an un/thing

      one more flight   from trauma

after i found out he had been fucking other women all along, more than anything i wanted to know if they could interrupt his stony exterior & were they beautiful on the one hand i am so sexually possessive as to feel i might die if i am not the one place where all of a man's cum journeys; on the other i expect nothing & accept less than nothing

in the aftermath i tell people i left him bc he couldn't love me & this is a truth

although not the whole one

there are no such things that exist as true stories

there is the story u tell & the thing which happened

& neither are especially real

i love narrative

i suck on every tale like a hard candy

until it reveals its innards to my salivating tongue

i am always starving & i never eat   not really

i am a girl in a fairy story   my stomach is the stone

of a philosopher   it transforms everything inside of me

i would like the story that i am telling u to be verifiable

bc i know by now what kind of a girl u think i am

if i expose my   self exhaustively enough

will i be believed or;   merely   embarrassed

i write a poem that is the words *i am embarrassed*

& nothing else   repeated endlessly

for 10 entire pages   i could reproduce

it here but u get the idea—   u grow tired   ;

in a way shame is the great leveler

& i've been in shoddier boats

[fri jul 24]

in the last month i've found my self overwhelmed

preoccupied w the recent exes   also w the memory

of one unspeakable face

a man who has reappeared a half-dozen times during the shutdown

that early march night before the bars closed his eyes boring on hart street
once more into mine

that annihilation

spine gone rigid   (rigid   from *rigere*   to be stiff
                              as in death   as in rigor mortis

            as in it was not the first time

         i was made dead   but it was the worst)

was there a re/cognition   there

in my face did he too see   that night

or am i   one more passing ship

past plugging holes   sinking my   self

i flog my   self   this bad orientation

that is   ;   toward only the fragmenting   pasts

the reckonings   o my god   where pleasure

on the floor of my bathroom   i heave & cannot

take in breath   worry now   of the global disease

hyperventilating all through the night

pulling bra & panties on

in case by morning i am a body   bereft

       abandoned of personhood

NEVER BE FOUND NUDE

& yet   i live

*

preoccupied   yes

perhaps bc of our moving in a week

leaving the brooklyn apartment i've spent the longest time in; the only to
have felt like a home

packing away the detritus of four years' worth of relationships

also the   break   down   & yet i live

find his coat   or the other's watch   condoms unused &
past their expiry

an exposure of the interior to his totality

        one more mistake

an insinuation of love

which was only ever a haunting   & yet   i live

butler   again: *even the Other who brutalizes me has a face*

butler   citing levinas: precisely *the Other who persecutes me
has a face*

              i will see *that* man's face

        forever unto death

in the levinasian sense of the intersubjective encounter it is that foundational exposure of one's necessary face to the other that creates an ethical precondition of our being

a responsibility

i do feel responsible

i blame   my   self

for everything

[mon aug 3]

today we moved

today my essay on tranny chasers went live

will i ever write of anything but me me me me me me me me me—
that is;

> in the context of whether or not i am fuckable   (i am)

i know i am a bad girl

but baby i love u

if i write of my life i am asked when i will put my head in the oven

i say i cannot be sure but it isn't especially the way i would choose to shuffle
off

i wonder if anyone asked ted hughes about the ethics of *birthday letters*

i wonder if anyone asked robert lowell what elizabeth hardwick thought of *the
dolphin*

it strikes me that for woolf   plath   & sexton   entire histories
become the incidental *shit* of titillating teleologies of suicide

next time a man asks u about hysteria lick ur lips & recite

benjamin

berryman

hemingway

mayakovsky

thompson

foster wallace

in hell they'll all call me mommy

i'm j kidding   baby

i'm going to heaven

i am asked by a poet friend about my *training*—my *formal approach* & i say
i thought it rather obvious i have none

        or;

        this is partly true

i have training in the reading of poems; but little in the writing of them

also;   i am disinterested in formalism   *bad girl*

i say i think it is perfectly right there are poets to whom we look for son-
nets, ghazals, sestinas, & the like

also to the inventors! i think, recently, of jericho brown's astonishing
duplexes in *the tradition*; jos charles' radical refashioning of middle english
in *feeld*

it is possible i could become another sort of a poet

is free verse dead

well is it

still i find it indispensable for me to encounter the splattering of the sort
of work i feel alive in making

in life i am often treated as a freakish intervention in the mundanity of
the lives of others

i love the friction of feeling as if i might wrench control of this sensation
to produce such

        interruptibles

i suppose it is entirely possible that the thing that i am is decidedly not a
poet

or;   is it right that i name my   self   such

i have little national feeling; little investment in the costuming of identity categories—be they personal or else professional; et cetera

i detest tribalism of any sort

so;   am i a bad girl; a bad poet—both;   or ; neither

[sun may 10]

if i were good i would render my writing more obtusely

i would write as if my mouth were full

of mfas   rather than dicks

then i could be in [redacted] magazine

& make one trillion dollars

pay to get my face done   pussy

done   teeth   done

i don't know if i could turn down that cia money & i know this is one
reason i am so so so so so so so so so so so so so so so so bad

i remember telling my ex-boyfriend i could never go back to sex work

but i have always been the sort of girl who would do anything

to have one more day   even only another hour

on this wondrous earth

[sat aug 1]

that i long to be good does not entail a necessary satiation of the desire

does desire only ever subsist in its own hollowing

                        is its face blank as god's

it has always seemed to me that for men   satisfaction snuffs need out
 or;

initiates escalation procedures

as in a fast & furious movie   where each successive iteration requires
wider & wilder explosions

in plainer terms

there is no greater mistake than giving a man the thing he longs for

most especially if the thing that he longs for is u

i can't speak for other women

my desire reproduces its self in its self

as if through binary fission—is endless

       & i need i need   i need   i tire

       of oxygenating my   self

give me all of u or flee me

god i feel time is dissolving   & am in terror

i see death cavorting in each oak leaf;

i cannot cease in the manner of my life

i would guzzle the universe in its entirety like spring's first warm sun
or; come

i would choose eternal life

if only to wiggle my toes in each grain of sand on this earth

to love each astonishing person

      for their *one big self*   ;

        {also to read every book}

i am trying, unsuccessfully, to locate the source of a nadine gordimer re-mark—*perhaps the best way to write is to do so as if one were already dead*—but find only advertisement-infected sites which collate celebrity quotes, & also a mention of it in a terry gross interview w the late author

sometimes i fear my brain is filled w snippets of other writers' work which insinuate themselves into my dailinesses but which i will never locate again

i have for example been searching my shelves for heather christle's *crying book* but must have lent it out or lost it in the move; or else, it is in some strange nook of the new apartment & i have in turn lost the trail of engage-ment i wished to make w it

i think how every bit of reading or writing i snatch away is from out of the hands of death; that is, i hadn't expected to be alive as long as i have & now feel everything i do or make occurs in the *after-the-fact* of a kind of life

i have been writing as if i were already dead

or as good as

but then, laughing, i realize i have mapped only trauma onto the quote—my forever propensity—& have forgotten the latter half, where gordimer goes on to say *afraid of no one's reactions, answerable to no one's views*

& the fact is i likewise elude these fears perhaps for the same reasons

i am unworried by the prospect of being disrespected by poets! of all things!

i only worry over the possibility of dying w/o having been loved well

in any case i tell a poet-friend that i do not anticipate ever being a poet's poet; i know already which position i occupy in the limited imaginary in which i am known; & do not care! my work connects w those who read & love it & they reach out to say they feel deeply in it, as i feel this is all that ever matters to me about the work

i don't need to fundamentally alter the world   or;

      perhaps not in this context

the world is ending around me

i only wish to offer some small window of connection or comfort

i only wish to regard everyone on the level of their whole selves & to love
those i am able

                      *

still

i detest cynicism above all else!

i worry this is how i sound

i only mean that the work is best contextualized in action & experience

i want to be good in the sense   too   that i *do* leave the
world better than i came into it

& think of my poems not as trifles but as love letters to those who seek
them

& that i believe poetry might change the world; has changed mine & that
i also have other work to do, other loving; other *being withs*; & do not
require entrenchment in any establishment, for, i think, what has such
anchoring ever done for the good of all

[¿¿¿]

why is it i am always thinking of rhoda in *the waves*

stopped dead before the puddle

unable to step over   that mirrory pool

who should part their legs not i   not i   not good

girls in frocks   flocking toward

an inexorable   unraveling of time's yarns   the tide

tugs the sand from the shore like nails clawing a back

it is bleeding   itself out   the black sheen

of the water under moonlight   gone solid

the primordial soup of this life   sucks & pulls

a sloppy blowjob   all cummy   w sufferance   sticking

in ur hair   on ur tits   & in the tear ducts   crusting over

      i long for a looser language of the body

a method of disarticulating   limbs from history

& history   —from u

in some other bubble universe

i am a girl still   & unbent   still plucking blooms
                                       from stems

in abandon   & the yellow under my chin whispers

                    he loves me

red petals of hollyhocks or geraniums simply will not

do   o   *he loves me not*

& the white blossoms

        float up in my basin

i am determining the possibility of a face

i am no longer one   &   am exposed

of *the waves* woolf noted in her diaries that the book (*an elegy*, one thinks, rather than a novel) came like a *fin in the waste of waters which appeared to me over the marshes out of my window at rodmell when i was coming to an end of* to the lighthouse

*

no matter how many times i read up on her natal chart i inevitably convince my self by the next time i look into it that woolf must have been a pisces; but no, a january 25th birth, an aquarius after all; w an air-dominant chart, & a great number of taurean (my sun sign) placements

not infrequently i visit astrotheme.com to look over birth chart readings for dead writers & dead celebrities; it is both disorienting & amusing to me that the substance of the text there speaks of these people as if they are still living, & usual

virginia woolf, the diurnal south-eastern quadrant, consisting of the 10th, 11th, & 12th houses, prevails in your chart: assertions & goal achievements are at the centre of your concerns

cheers for communication & mobility, virginia woolf!

your natal chart shows a lack of the water element, w only 0.00% instead of the average 0.25%! whether you are aware of it or not, affective values bring about problems, for you or your friends

*

ofc i know why i am preoccupied w rhoda in *the waves*; have chewed on that cud for a decade

she draws out woolf's terror of sexual embodiment; the trauma of the social body; the self-protective dissociational impulse; she is indeed imagined in the text by louis as *having no body as the others have*

& the form of the book itself a kind of miscellany to return to for comfort in the production of my own sequence of pastiche

from the diaries, again: *what interests me* [...] *was the freedom & boldness with which my imagination picked up used & tossed aside all the images & symbols which i had prepared. i am sure that this is the right way of using them—not in set pieces, as i had tried at first, coherently, but simply as images; never making them work out; only suggest. thus i hope to have kept the sound of the sea & the birds, dawn, & garden subconsciously present, doing their work underground*

*

virginia woolf, the choice is yours: love encountered...

*

[sun mar 22]

the precarity of placing my/ self

again   in the hands of strange men

perhaps i grow more fearful w age

each new fuck   a lock turning

a few weeks ago a patron told me

he loved what a little slut i am & i

said *what do u mean* & he said

wearing all that *behind the bar*

grabbing those bottles

& i think but do not say that i am

merely fulfilling the basic duties

of one more shitty job in the clothes

i feel comfortable wearing that are movable

& breathable   & help me to bring in tips

later i acquiesce to a nightcap

he slides his hand up my skirt

     there is always a hand sliding up my skirts

     there is always a man who needs me

     to be his little slut   his little hole

he will not save me

& i cry when i crawl into bed   & to what end

mine

[¿¿¿]

i have lived too long under the delusion   that i will be
        loved

but this is not the fate of the bad girl

it is a matter of the chromosomal

no   i shall go up in smoke

skin   fat cracking   crazed pope joan

or;   saved by freeze frame

some flame flying over a cliff

a 1966 thunderbird dissolves in thin air

my hair whipping   foxtail behind me

the lovely curve   to cross   knowledge

of that line   of beauty   possible only in death

the world flattens & scowls

     i am taken out of time

placed in *no-place*;   this is feminist iconography

the good girl exists only in contradistinction to her dark twin

the convertible oriented toward nothing again again again again again

[???]

every thing i write is something i should not have written

if i were good i would not be so saturated by shame

it thickens my blood   like flour   i am sluggish   i wish

i knew another sort of being   i wish i would write

poems of joy   &   beauty   i wish

i had a river so long   i would teach my feet to

fly   why is joni   intervening here

will i see my mother at christmas this year

& will this book break her heart

how to be a good girl

value the ~~openings~~

~~of ur chambers~~   good girl

~~no more leaving room for jesus~~

the man carves ~~a headboard from a cross~~

& breaks ~~it~~   pumps ~~pumping~~   into u

          gas station

      type girl   ~~cheap garters from rainbow type girl~~

     wondrous sluttery
the bedframe turns ~~& turns & turns~~

       legs part~~ing~~ in perpetuity

           o baby

seal everything   door   key

hole   window too   a shroud ~~of duct tape~~

~~should do~~   ~~some~~ lost Turinian fascinator

fashion ~~forward thinking~~ requiring dissolution

     of personae

     ~~& the self w it~~

although the air u exhale is lovely   ~~yes~~

~~precious~~   ~~also~~ lavender   o

they shall make of u a diamond in the end of things

crushed carbon ~~u must~~ understand it is necessary

to be so small   subatomic

darling   ~~this is the long route to love~~

u are the spell in the cave

~~that~~   ~~o~~ recitation of desire

surrender self-preservation

~~it is the~~ narcissistic ego

-investment of the bad girl ~~& u ?~~   u

are a young ~~little~~ temple thing

the accoutrement of a god a king

fucks u once   says *throw it in w the rest*

               ~~o u doll~~

          entombation

is a process of love   a decontext

-ualization   ancient useless knowledge

~~the business~~ of no-dick-game-having-historians

an instruction ~~to the world~~ concerning ur worth

how to be a good girl

~~start by being unqualified~~
~~to write such instruction manuals~~

~~has it come time to cop to failure~~

i am an awful decadence
i fill w the shrillness of ~~tackiest~~ sunsets
i am childless   ~~& shall be~~
i am ~~an~~ the inconsideration ~~at the center~~ of a ~~far flung~~ galaxy
little light left emitting
i am its dulled womb
a hysterectomy of planetary magnitude
i am aching tits & god
-full as i should like to be

i do not understand prayer
except w a beautiful cock in front of me

should He allow me to live in grace or;
despair   i think (bad girl)   perhaps
it is no insurmountable pass between here & there
i desire   i genuflect

i big big big bang ~~o daddy~~

i beg for more

how to be a good girl

~~u are a proliferation of concessions~~

~~u tilt ur head & the sun flares & burbles~~

~~u spit shine shoes w ur pink tongue~~

~~& when u widen ur terrible maw u~~

never say no

[tues sept 1]

i adore an overgrown garden

i would like dandelions

intertwined w amaranth

w morning glories & goose

grass   also the bluebells

      better to know the names of flowers

than to confess   *girlishly*

      that i am ignorant   *of nature* (sontag)

i adore this hodgepodge book

drafts   & diary bits bursting

like weeds   there are only so many

times u can be told that u are too much

before i am too much i am too much i am

too much i am too much i am too

in my horror at the possibility of this going to press i consider deleting
everything—the book; the backups; the emails w their coterie of phantoms

i get high   soothe my   self

remind   —self

even if a failure it will have been a beautiful one

like life

II.

a   the
ramble   poem

...

for me, dread only

i may stop knowing
how to like and desire
the world around me

EVE SEDGWICK
A DIALOGUE ON LOVE

how to be a good girl

first off u get born

        that awful happening

        that rib from the trunk   of an undeliberate

                                      man

        that bodying

        that unfurling   into some context

ur ass is slapped   u are a raw chicken   wading

placental   out   out   of the obsidian

belch of nothingness   all softs a raw

something   awaiting assignation

                a somewhere to get to

the doctor knows u   by the undulating warble

of need's honing missile   such wailing!

for a world's opening   & which cry

rising from ur wet sudden mouth

producing such swirling squid-ink!

should attest to novel materiality—

        the attendants

            sigh & marvel at these tectonics

which is it   love

        which speaks

we are trying on a voice   shouldering a face

in the dressing room   know

we are in the origin story now

u will be awarded some bow; ribbon;   somesuch

sequence of pink cleavings

        & so

in the sterilized austerity of the birth-event

u are to be given over

to a tragedy of the biological

our inciting trauma   a formulation of form

that initiation into the confoundment of whatever

it is the academics are calling modernity   ; these days

everywhere squirreling

dead books   dead hightowers

those bottlenecking tenure minions

guarding it all   in sickness   or in another

        sickness   o

the generational hoard   cerebral

hoard   this hoarding of resources   is never

                    merely a question

            of the tactile

what do u call a public intellectual

i seem to have forgotten the punchline to my joke

they are hoarding my laughter
my snake hair wriggles & withers
            beneath their inspecting eyes
which have been propped up   ;   which appear
                                divested
                rotating & singular
                        which appraise
the fill of the examination room
            pontificating
on a certain constitution of the subject   :   i
am swallowed up   a bolus gulped
into the thicket of the overused throat
now sing little birdie *sing sing*
it is here where the thing that is becoming this *i*
is found   in any case there is this body
a case of u   the marble-filled jar
we are all betting on
the body   as it were   is a girled one
& we girl & writhe under the mantle
of an ineluctable subordination

                        so buck up   baby

        it is a time

on a clock here   melting

                           a time

        for an undoing

now begin again

no chicken   u

chickee   subsequent to the devastation

of the egg   drooping   slimily

into the ceramic bowl of the attenuating world

there is a batter of possible

womanhood   there   readied

for the baking   this burgeoning self

        must be maneuvered inside

our sheet cake of geologic disintegration

                    now

                        integrate ur self

        love

lap at the sugars in which u are encased

taste   sicksweet   history

of frosted & swanning girlhood

        what   girlhood

one more loss to the emulsifications

                of time jutting up

        against its own

                            shortening

                time

u think

        tugging ur mask from ur mouth   lamenting

how to kiss the staled air of this city

u love & which is disinterested

also quieter now noise   or;

       its contexts one more signal

       of risks to be managed

unraveling in the lately of whatever damned year

               this is   & whatever happened

       to new york minutes   time   yes   lost

       to apocalyptic revelations

of our solitudinous present

           like a quarter which bears its neutral weight

against a dud of a scratch ticket   revealing

       an aloneness   which was there before   always

          just spackled over in the obtuseness

             of the everydayness   the mundanity

              of the just-my-luck

      of the outcome we wished finally

                           to avoid

         & in turn that flailing of who we are

      never becoming

though the longing hangs

    there   licking its ghostly lips

          blowing kisses

toward a memory of the possible world

& were we living

or just laboring

just whittling at wooden clock turns   just standing

perhaps on the platform in perpetuity

the a train taking forever

the j train taking forever

the g train may never come

did the animals know themselves to be all alive

before their names had been placed—

wafers atop adam's tongue

before   as it were   their manufacture

o love   & do we persist only in the wanting

is a life a life in name alone

lord   *this endless wanting*

      this boundless insistence on naming it

      recognize

the singular power wielded by the good girl   *desire*

& does she need or is she merely required

      ornamentally...

in julia leigh's 2011 directorial debut *sleeping beauty*, emily browning plays a young (*promiscuous*, according to the film's wikipedia entry) university student (lucy) in need of money, who takes a position as a niche call girl, wherein she is voluntarily sedated in an especially luxe brothel & fondled in her sleep by male clients while her employers observe & film the encounters

it seems crucial to note that vaginal penetration is not allowed in these encounters

it seems crucial to note that lucy is denied permission to view the tapes

it seems crucial to note that she surreptitiously films the final encounter of the narrative anyway & in which encounter the client overdoses & lucy lies beside the corpse unawares

female looking is ofc to be punished

      bad girl

when i was a child i watched the disney sleeping beauty over & again each dull week

& think now how the leigh variation makes explicit the tale's eroticization of female helplessness—

in the tradition of countless folkloric erotic fixations

       & think how that fairy story was always a narrative   of rape—
       how in some   versions, the king   impreg
       nates beauty as she sleeps

       & she is woken not w a kiss—but w the suck of her   newborn's
       mouth at her   finger—pulling that terrible splinter
       from flesh;   breaking its untoward   magic

the man of course   no where to be found

& beauty saddled w her colicky grief babies

her fixed star decided

& what moral   for the young girl

neither fall spelled nor slumber

nor ever ever be born at all

& i suppose one question might be

what would u do for enough money

to sustain a life   in a tough city

o god   this city spits   girl's need back

as a crashing wave spits out some slack foot

again;   wrecked   on some shell-littered shore

          or other   or; else

the usual solvents to new york's particular lonesome

are vanished now   o

those dazed nights

quick fucks   bad blow

the endless slurring marching

of bars bars bars   bars on my windows suggestive

of an inside/outside dualism   another fiction

another marker of space;   or property;

the good girl placed   in the gauze interior

          protected   where she shall silently pray

               to what

the man at the park across franklin ave today

his body bejeweled in signs & symbols

of what one hopes must be a less disengaged god

than the one watching over us

& pray to the bodies of beautiful men

whistling   straying past as i write this   their struts

          so unpracticed   unfearful

          no headphones in

                              just vibes

& i have to say there are corners   also

days where the girl-soul loses substance

fails to establish its self

      the soul   ; or the subject

      or;   i pray to understand

boundedness   i am w/o   inside

or out   am diffused   in light

& scared   revealed

to be a conflagration of particulate

stacking upon particulate

which assumes a falsely particular visage

yes   o

if i am outside   i must be quiet as a mouse

so as to hide unnoticed   so as to avoid the inspection

i am   i am   i am

     a bright

     a shimmering

     heat rising from a hood

     i am a visual hallucination

     a list of possible endangerments

like any girl   & if i only knew

how to be good   i would vibrate too

along a safer frequency   perhaps i would stay out

of the news   i might pray   to an angel;

a patron saint of dead women   abused women

         there are so many

      scattered

   iconographies   of a dozen dozen boneyards

     & is it the case of the modern girl

     in some more universalizable sense

     that she is

     mere accumulate

     manufactured of the dead

     a titillation   some trash

     -heap   of our various personhoods /

        disregarded   ;

  this   :   our compost soil of Woman

     i want to tell u

            {but shouldn't}

     we are growing wilder

     we stamen & petal   sun-doomed

       decaying in shine

        braining

          in some sill

     devising a precarious logos

  touching things   forbidden

learning

what epistemology   this   ;   of the good girl

what edificatory circumstance is opening

for u   what gospel   who shall teach u

how to be a good girl   who snap

the ruler across ur milk-knuckles   my bunny

there are no saints   sainting in their hollows

after all   nor patronizing

the travels of good girls   through shaded woods

alleyways   or houses   where daddies

disrobe themselves of their fatherly duties

as one shucks an oyster

where agnes   where maria   where mary & all the rest

just take a survey of the damned

                    statistics

a girl's life is infinite

-ly corruptible   or;

should such mixed messaging suffice

do we shock   or;   bear witness

this metaphor of one more cut up darling

the world adores a dead girl   ; we shore our longings up

                    aspire in getting

dead   done for   it is a placing in the archives

it is a becoming

soluble w/in the echoing

of the memory cave

or   ;   will they query   these words

their own uselessness

the poet's blunder

what is an *actionable* utterance   a word

;   please

remind it it may not speak its self

what authority has it   what larynx   what voice

in the maw

or;

the address animates the subject into existence

thus i speak my   self   or;   am spoken into being

if language can sustain the body

it can also threaten its existence

what philosophies!   what silt in the throat!

a good girl mouth shall part only for the looking

or;   we return to our lessons

& u are learning

should u look upon it

the god-eye is smooth   tumbled   some

store-bought stone or salt-lick   & the mute

mirrory gaze

of its blank is reflecting

only u back to u   elaborating

       ur lack   the cake

collapsing undramatically in the oven

& u again w it

where now   god   or;   nothing

i should like to face facts

i should like to wrestle

ur indifference   how biblical

     such familiar sensation

indifference   in the clocktower looms

a sort of a man after all!

time to toss that vest patch out

proclaim!

i have looked upon the creator   are we well-met

no woman   no nothing   another hashtag

     for the rubble of dull

     star-deadened *experience*

& is the future Female

or   ;   are we in the end of History

unwatched   unattended

or   ;   should we be this Future

in current projections

are we thus commemorated

again   harbingers of more death

as in   death is in the apple

as in   all four horsemen   donning tits

                                              ass   pussy hats

is the final girl

-boss   merely some manifestation

of the mark of the beast   o

god   how are we

so inevitably accountable for these Falls   or the others

in the end of whatever

this thing we call *life*   persists

                    unfortunately

           in becoming

& is every such platitude one more failure

each phraseology imbricated   only in

                              more

                    shame

a longer path toward the impregnation

of the self   w its poison

internalized investment in articulations of our own improbable goodness

some gold-dusting of belladonna

across the granite countertops of every aspirationalist barbie dream home

                          o social climber

have u killed god   vanished that original perpetrator

now we must turn the sharpening snaketongue of animosity inward

the woman's out!

viciousness in the kitchen!

& another poetess in the oven

burning her damned head off

as the children laugh

milk spoiled   bread molded

the tape about the door jamb pulling away from its edges

                           like old polish chipping

        back from the cuticles of a dry dead finger

the cake in any case fallen

settling into its self   like an aged matriarch

rocking on a porch   wrinkling in the sun

which is   as we know   getting hotter

              or else;   god help;   we are

        barely edible now scrawled over

in the loveless lettering of a billion billion eons

of cosmological grief

what stuttering inheritances we suffer!

what slack stooping of the spine

over dustpans & flaccid cocks

& in my place on hands

knees   my arms bend back

my nails pull from their beds

in the sweet grand stink of cleaner

& another cry to attend to

in which cavity does the utterance originate

& who the addressee

is it u   me   me   or me

the good girl is   like any other positionality

constitutively drawn in the relational encounter

for ex.

eve to her original man

to his great god   & man to his beasts

or;   a real housewife to camera two

            the confessional booth

me to u to u to u to u

lap at my longing

i should flay my   terrible self   in full view

of a star's photospheric surface if it please u

if i only could be good

such clapping

of hands   asses

i in my housedress   outclassed again   crying

                                            for no one

        nothing   failing   to be

                      o

now let us gather our trailings & beg

-in   again

see

we are going on a trip   we are taking to the road

extrude arm from morass

avoid *more ass* joke

sell ass instead;   for;   no profit

in comedy   still;

the body is another thing all together

darling   come out now—leave the cake on the sill

hand goes first   that which marks

its own form;   may draw its self for consumption

i'm talking

bad girl

of the cannibal

imperative of the human

so

stop a moment

take stock   survey the horizon & consider

in sight of these shockingly rapid smoke signals

we are told *concessions must be made*

IN THESE TRYING TIMES

IN THESE WILD TIMES

IN THESE UNCERTAIN TIMES

IN THESE TIMES   new romans

burning another decadent iteration

of what or whom is having;

or else   ;   not

on twitter a woman asks

when will times be precedented again

& instead of ruminating on one more rhetorical

i shall masturbate four times

a day   moaning   vote

vote vote vote vote vote into my pillow

laughing   is this love   politicians

inform me my rote motions   acceptable only

muffled under white noise of silencers

so as to not disturb too greatly

the blur & suck of the contemporary

& i think   what knowledge do politicians have

of pleasure   ;   besides its theft

each ballot i am handed

is an apologia for rapes or lynchings or both

& there are things u can't fuck away

although i keep trying

but daddy   does a good girl talk

like i do   do i exceed my role   do i

need more than the possibilities of my representation

should i present the hole

        of my   self

shall i open my legs for this!

our false flag of democracy

sharpening its end

if i should leak   coral goes all white

i plug my   self w plastic straws   pour one out

for my dears in california packing their go-bags

though i think   is there anywhere left to get to

i say i should save u   but i can't seem to get out

        of my damned bed

so the hand journeys south   the hand wanders

& numbs   what is working from home

but one more exploitation   & i am getting close

should say   if there has been one brief blessing

i have been an exquisite engineer of my own pleasure

yet   here;   in repetition

is the orgasm losing   its glittering

particularity   or;   if a good girl cums

w no man to witness   did she even spasm   does the body

                              articulate its   self

          best through nerve-endings which tree-grasp

outwardly   i'm talking (*bad girl*)   of the crown

shyness of the senses   or;   is the body

but an end from its start   anne says

death too is in the egg

& we are cracking up

so i get high   i reach frailly

toward a moral creed   & for why

what greed in the throat!   fingers outstretched

little giraffe necks   this yearning adirectionality

               & say *enough brain-worming*

          & beg

in   again

we have forgotten our trip!

silence the oven-timer

which has been citing an ending for hours

to no one   or; nothing

leave wrecked   charred remains

                              of the self to cool

& step out   let's stroll   precarious

arrogant   sunning under

a roadside stupor   what more

maudlin than a hitchhiker's thumb stumped

in the breeze of this

our last expansionism   a tumbleweed

enters the frame   a touch

on the nose if u ask me (*u didn't*)

sad sack piano theme shit

imagine   incredible hulk   backpack

tracking back down   the endless

highway's endlessness   ended

westwardly-horny

side-eyed american progress &

it is time to decide what u are doing

                         girl

now begin again

there is a reason u have come here

u have a function u are lying

in wait   for what   edibility

o reach around

dust self delicately

in confectioner's sugar then

                wait

until lumbering He sways over

to ur supplicant splay

futurist nostalgia   cheesecake girl

one waist reducing   to a single point

on the joint axes of flesh & fantasia

            now push up

            into our collective unconscious these

torpedo tits   slather teeth w slick

grease   widening our war-effort grins

the girlboss returning   again   again

in an effort of *nation-building*

say i seem to have lost my way

say there is a podcast for that

say to the first car who brakes

that for some stretch of 700 dust-deadened miles

u adorn each rest stop bathroom & no mistake

                        baby   ur a star

the sky gulps its dark cartography & thins

now begin again

in such sluttish immensity of knowledge

that He shall snort as well as eat u

appraising ur form   shorn

of the protestations of the body

now   in his palm   honey

                are u fish scale

                        ur iridescences mutter

sonnets

            addressed to no one

                    dithering no where   rooting in nothing

& nothing rooted but this exhaust-blanketed stretch of tar He paints to
blank

u are as any good drug

u are as any good girl

whole men pen roadtrip records

attest to the dull fact of what u have

been   but the song has skipped

hike up ur bra   perk tits   perk ears

recite a dylan   it doesn't matter which

it's called *method*   baby

the Man is noticing how u are noticing now

the needle's fumbled its track

there is a failure in the fulcrum

of history   it is us

though we set out

the highways will be plugged

makeshift trenches are getting dug

           up for *you know what*

& there may be no after

it comes time

to tell it like it is

we are facing an ending   gazing

upon the cessation of the event

shall we self-quarantine in time beyond time?

in this continuance of plagues?

there may be a fork here

an overgrowth   or else

some inconspicuous signage

cleaving the horizon

it bides time   tender & solitary

one more mark of heaven

for the damned to stumble over

pointing   which way

to mercy   through the foothills

over the crick   & past the sea

what geography

this?   the girl loses land

or finds it peopled   evilly & at end;

He returns

inhale   be flipped

like a pancake & widened

u think how possible u have been

& are no more   shall u

engulf the speculum

of the other woman   or;

the engine turns;

the good girl is filled

w knowing   traces

some infiniteness   no map-minder

she   ;   transmogrifies   ;   colloidally

each pitstop her becoming

now think back   recall

never get lost in thought

at a rest stop   doll

gape-mouth draws more flies

in inattention

but do not take me at my word

there is no trick less certain

than the utterance

          yet still i purge

       & still grow thin skin   bones   the like

the good girl is   how do u say   an excavation

i cannot stop

i runneth over

i am off-roaded

there is no help in it

i blame my   self   for everything

now grant me

       daddy

a thieved moment

to be the bad girl

press my lips to rearview

leave there a candied kiss   is this love

       this wet intake of breath

i'd never dream of   this slick

of my thighs

imprints   in my dreams

a leather interior of my own making

i think (*bad girl*)

i should like to have been born

facilitated   outside

the manufacturer's standards

i should like to know

the weightlessness of a lost rover

in space   i may float!   i may go up!

aimless   in my sheath of interstellar debris

impearled in light   & starred forever

free as i'd like to be

picture   that stretch

of 95 where the cops' hide-

y-holes   are smoked past

& there   left over

a solid 30 miles of leafed bliss

bare foot on dash   chipped

crimson polish   smoke dangling

from corner of crimson

mouth   its own scandal

          of particularity

singular promise of throat's softest flesh

i require ontological lubricant!

the girl's desire exists!   & she too;

in such intercessions

& yeah ok

each time i'd play

joni's *case of u*—

        its spell—

its fingerpicked

need   disarticulated

from any particular man

a woman   i

would lie to my own damn self

about the range of my voice

singing w her   reaching for notes

sun in my mouth sun on my throat

sun tickling my teeth   then the uvular joy

my molars could shout!   my hair

whips through humid air

choking the rest of virginia out

but we are curving a bend!

we molt & gather!

the low knell of locusts unfurls

seventeen underground years of sirening set loose

for one last summer   in ocher heat

it resonates less behind the paywall

such awful humming before god

meted out between ads for snake oil

flat tummy tea   ; some nights under lee of sleep

my dreams run east-west   have eight lanes

name themselves 64   i think i too was a girl

once   it's no good waking   but i do

days are worse

i writhe alone in my bed

another hum beneath my throw

small blessings   o my god

i tell Him if it all goes up

he has to get to brooklyn

        say

he'll huff juniper   ambergris   myrrh & mint

        say

i need him to fuck me before i go

in his beaked mask   beneath his glassy sight

        say

he may lay his cock like a coin over mine eyes

        say

to the last among us that *now u have witnessed*

the funeral procession of the good girl

stop

how

do i say

i'm not ready to die

in a poem

i think i just did

promises weigh my tongue

they are sapphires   indigo

silencers   i roll

them over my teeth

        got grit in ur mantle girl

who cares for damaged enamel

or prophecy   more grecian mess   ;

so much for oracles in this—

whole world a damned Pompeii

i should anoint my   self

i should bunker down

i would like to be covered in cum

        one last time

i bathe as gods bathe

i vibrate smilingly

i take longer than 20 seconds

the philosopher inquires

do good girls dream

of obedient sheep

& the record cuts

kuhkuh kuhkuh kuhkuh kuhkuh

the moon like an opal regards u   an achievement

now be ingested   darling

u are learning what it is to be loved

it is a planetary terror

it is a gargling of galaxies

III.

a

loving

the

dream of life

...

*If blue were not blue how
could love be love.*

C.D. WRIGHT
"IMAGINARY MORNING GLORY"

[tues sept 1]

a year to the day since i last saw j

what does a good girl recall   crumpled

down comforter   a dream of lying perfectly still

in pampas grass   a hand's grip on my hips

that last day the sudden thunderstorm

          so ham-handed!

standing in the rain   w me in his coat

& the car he'd called for me waiting

kissing quiet; some romcom cliché on the cutting-room floor

i tried to remember the color of his eyes the other day &

                    found my   self

relieved that i couldn't

[weds sept 2]

terribles work their way into me & are coated in nacre;

gather time about them like a shawl & harden—

my little griefs & small labors   my pearls

what is sorrow

it is a life

it is

[thurs sept 3]

a woman yells into her cell on the sidewalk in front of my apartment

at first i am annoyed; she's been shouting since before i began prepping dinner & now it is finished, dishes done, & i'm sipping a red wine which is about to turn while jotting my little sillinesses at my desk

the woman's voice: husky, sensuous, a sound of still water parting around a body

i realize suddenly that she is begging a lover

      for what

i feel badly but i cut off my window unit to better hear her

LET ME GO   *LET ME GO*   *LET ME*

        LIVE MY LIFE

[redacted], it's been two years!

can't u hear that i am hurting   *can't u*

hear   *i am in pain!*

i can hear it

i wish i could take her hand in mine; ease her burden in some way; i wish [redacted] would let her go

also; this is none of my business

also; everyone's hurt hurts me

also; i would like to help & can't

        *

kate bush singing *i am sick of love* in "song of solomon"

that's it; that's the moment

*

[fri sept 4]

i can't seem to work out where u have come from

still   here u are in me   & i;   here;   o

i think how in brooklyn *what are ur cross streets* is an erotic inquiry

& w/o anticipating this, w/o anticipating anything at all, quite suddenly

my cross streets are wherever ur dick hardens

mine are the place of a moon whose face is too wide & proud for the sky;
the way u point it out to me as if we are the first to have ever noticed her
lolling about up there

& we are

oh my god   my cross streets are u asking *yeah?* in response to my
whimpers   my mouth parts   my breath catches on the hook of ur rhythm

think again of the balm of nikky finney's voice intoning *repetition is holy*

& say   stay   here; stay here; stay   here;   stay

[mon sept 7]

i text to tell u i'm touching myself again

today i've come 6 times   so far

each time it's ur expression when i wrap my wet hands around ur cock i'm
dreaming of

tomorrow i see u again; can barely confine my need

u say to me i used the word *insatiable* & i remind u i also said that i feel i
am a bitch in heat for u

i need u to cum in me three billion billion times & seventy-six more for
good measure

i want to wade through a sea of ur come   drown in it
          entirely smug   clam-happy

i am vacillating between cum/come bc i notice u use *come* like a fancy man
& it turns me on how wholly unpornographic it is   how unamerican
          its crasslessness

i send u a dodie bellamy *cunt-up* bc i need u to know it is unfathomably
romantic to me to tell u i could die for one of ur loads

dodie: *unusually charged tonight, i sit here rubbing with vague smiles about
nothing, you fucking   me*

dodie: *i had no mouth, so your body said Be Here Now*

dodie: *i'm collapsing romance and porn*

dodie: *she no longer remembers these disembodied shreds of desire as her text*

who is the mistress of my desire? surely not i

[mon sept 14]

what i mean when i say i need to be full of u is don't discard me please

we are only j getting to know one another & my whole body aches for u all day long my heart baby it aches

when i tell u i want to get G O O D G I R L knuckle tattoos to commemorate the publication of this book u sigh in pleasure; say *that's so hot*

i am in a terror u will lose sight of me before we fall for one another properly & learn our way home

the writing process for this book has been a sort of devastation   that said   i delight in the possibility of its becoming a love letter in these, its death rattles; last pages

i want to [redacted] u & pray u might [redacted] me

at 11:11 twice per day all week i wish for [redacted]

i don't need any of this before god j take me to city hall i don't give a fuck

each time i text u i am brought to the edge of orgasm immediately

what is the freudian term?

u render me polymorphously perverse

my entire radius hums & buzzes   i am an electricity

i want to fall asleep w ur pubes stuck to mine & ur spit on my tits & tomorrow i will i will i will i will i will o

[tues sept 15]

an hour from now ur picking me up on ur motorcycle to take me on an adventure through queens

perhaps i will say

when my mother was a decade younger than i am now, she rode on the back of a beautiful man's motorcycle & ended up pierced through the fat & muscle of the thigh, through the femur, by a tree's branch

perhaps i will say   instead

that my mother   that day   learned to fly

& was reminded of the failure which privately bides its time in each & all our bodies

the body's orientation toward its own eventual undoing

& w this in back of my mind still i'll climb behind u & hold on to ur waist as if unkillable

are we bad women;   bodily dismantled

by men   & reconfigured   bionic

                    bolt-legs   & bud breasts

hog-tied   arrowed   defaced

saint sebastian as a girl to the tune of bjork's *venus as a boy*

i would be roped to a poplar

& run through

if it meant a certainty of being loved by u

*

branches which surface from our limbs

as novel limbs themselves

i love a story of trans

-formation   love a story of love

which kills   or close to it

we are not the first women to become trees

we are not the first women to die

we are a story

repeated

we fly   sustain;   or fail

still my mother lived

as did i

the sun blooms like a wound

i lick it w my pink tongue

& weep

i read that the balance & warmth of the composition of rubens' *saint sebastian healed by angels* (1601–1602) is characteristic of his italian period, his preoccupation w the classical world

but i know little, formally speaking, about painting

all i ever know in this life is if i am moved; or else, not

what i see is a nude & injured man prodded by winged cherubs

which is i suppose something one might desire in death

this being bathed in the regard of holy beings

the angels who attend him wear his face   his hair

& although the painting concerns his healing it is unclear to me in the perspective of the painting that they are removing his binds, extracting the arrows; the lack of visual motion, his slack face, may as easily indicate that the angels themselves pierce & tie him—perhaps little devils after all! or perhaps we are given to understand the angels may fail us, may fall in their goodness, might have their own motives, can act as bringers of death

the lord works in mysterious ways

et cetera;

[weds sept 16]

still—

wrapped, helpless, about ur entirely solid body on the back of ur motorcycle i think to myself *i'm j like the protagonist of rachel kushner's* the flame-throwers!

except not in charge—

& u my devilish communist   ;

my king in a world where there shall be no kings

at a stop light u reach back to rub my thigh & tell me what a good girl am i

i think i could die...fulfilled; my body warms & melds to urs as we sharply turn

in flushing we wander through a crowded intersection, an empty mall, & dine outside on an otherwise empty patio on hot squid, pickled cabbage, & blood soup; talk as lovers talk; that is, we say nothing of substance at all

u place ur sunglasses on my face & i take photos; one of each of us wearing them

i feel i haven't smiled—not really—in a thousand billion breaths; i am as a child now, i see the world all full of light

underneath the helmet i am an astronaut, vertigo'd—this strange feeling of soundlessness as if i have escaped gravity; my own intakes of air & exhalations—also; my necessary fear—the sole soundtrack

the lights on the kosciuszko bridge in the night now are stars shifting from fuschia to deeper violet to red, then green, gold; over & again

as we cross i trail the tips of my fingers over the buttons of ur shirt, slide them between the gaps there to tickle the pelt of hair which safeguards ur belly; i want to rest my cheek there, feel u grow hard again against my tits, to fall asleep w ur cock inside me—as if there were no other natural place for it to be

& there isn't

in bed, after, u ask me if i've read rachel kushner & i confess my earlier ridiculous love-thought; & we laugh & sigh, stupidly, in the way only those who have j fucked will do

*

later   i reach my fingers down   down

taste the salt of u leaking from me

& am returned to my home near the sea

        beach babies, the both of us

u tell me how u love it   love what   love

my filthiness   my need my need my need o god my need to have the
taste of our sex   the wet of us   our fluids which bleed & mix   on
my tongue also

this is the only communion w which i am familiar

krista tippett beginning each interview by asking the interviewee's religious
or spiritual background & practice

me answering in the above

that mingling in my mouth

this love its kind of rapture

full of u & contented i am, finally, safe

                    *

in the morning u leave ur spare helmet w me

so we won't worry about remembering

once u go i cannot help but weep   am

embarrassed   my weeping unfurls centuries

they glint & refract   & tell on themselves

in my way i am a statue of mary

w my wet eyes   seven sorrows & more still

i haven't cried in front of u yet & in this am proud

i am the strongest woman in the world & am good

the helmet faces me from the top of my dresser

w its blank stare   whispers *he will return*

even if only now bc u must

but i am trying to learn to trust u mean the things u say

i watch my plants sprout endless leaves this week

they are proximate to love   hear what we are & are alive

olive lay in ur arms this morning as i put on my makeup

u observed me   u & she each   smiling

velvet & privately bent;   in the mirror

i watch a girl photosynthesize   gauze

blossoms   heart-leaves   bolding   becoming
          in my hair

[thurs sept 24]

fort tilden today appears as a scene from *the road*; the shore emptied
of nearly all human bodies; the gulls having taken over, sentinels, their
throngs peppered here & again by common terns—whose bright red beaks
set them apart, strike my eyes, as i begin to discern their small number from
the remaining crowd

the sun throbs behind a gray haze; u say it may be the smoke from the
wildfires making its way to our horizon; certainly, it is colder today than it
has been, far colder than the perfectly hot day three weeks ago when i swam
out, out, & further out, entirely unperturbed by the water, & browning in
the sun

u slice & open a mango w ur hunting knife which i suck clean of its juices;
it is perfect, as we are, & sweet, as was the taste of me i'd discovered earlier
on ur mouth

when i straddle u, shivering, in my bikini, u slide ur fingers inside my bot-
toms & press them against my opening as i laugh & look about to be sure
the other stragglers aren't seeing where it is ur hands do wander

u tell me ur grandmother has seen a photo of me; has told ur mother that i
am cute & that we make a beautiful couple

it is here; in this moment; u say u don't wish to call me anything other than
ur girlfriend going forward & i sigh, relieved; feel as if i can breathe again;
as the waves crash violently & the fishermen clot on the wet sand some 20
meters down; this; our apocalyptic tableau

[sat sept 26]

in green-wood cemetery today we choose stuffy names for our children

augustus

letitia

cornelius & cornelia

hattie, nelly, crispin, & so forth

i make u store a copy of alison cobb's book in ur bike bag & we plan how we shall be buried here; choose our mausoleums; having decided, like little landlord fucks, to evict some of the current residents

i identify flowers as we wend our wild way hither, thither, & et cetera

the *grape leaf anemone*, a nuisance flower, but a beautiful one, originating in the himalayas; sturdy in windy conditions; thus its name from the greek, *anemoi*, the wind-gods

the *orpine*, a succulent perennial, w its densely-clustered flowers changing from blush to coppery-pink to rust w the progression of the blooming season; known too, in a fact i quickly kin to, as *witch's moneybags*

also the abundant beeblossom, beautiful & fragrant; also the rose fountain grass rustling its spiky inflorescences w the breeze; also the asiatic day-flower & baby's breath i tuck into my hair; also the horse chestnuts i carry happily home w us

my bike, when we return, w its sudden flat, which u assure me will be fine, noticing panic in my eyes; us 4 miles from home, & it getting late

but get home we do

i notice, achingly, i am already thinking of this as ur home too

[weds oct 7]

in the process of finishing a book on lovelessness, longing, & loss, i have managed a rather strange thing

i have fallen—unanticipatedly, quietly, quickly, wondrously—in love

    love

the great intangible (diane ackerman)

i don't know where we are getting to

but i could write another book for us;

indeed, shall write it, i pray

i went anxiously back & forth on whether or not to include this section in the manuscript, took an extra week past deadline to make the call, but felt, ultimately, that this book should end in beauty

i have often thought how plath's original ordering of the ariel poems begins w the word *love*—in "morning song"—& ends on the word *spring*—in "wintering," the close of her bee sequence

i think how in my life there has always been some small light, sustaining

it is entirely likely there is more pain in future, but i have always been the sort of woman to live, even if stupidly, in perpetual hope

i leave this book on such a note—in delight, w warmth, & in love—& w love for u all—xo, j

WORKS CITED, CONSULTED, OR OTHERWISE INDISPENSABLE TO THE BLOSSOMING OF THIS BOOK

diane ackerman, *a natural history of love*;

tori amos' 1996 record *boys for pele*;

roland barthes' *mourning diary & camera lucida*;

cunt-ups & *when the sick rule the world* by dodie bellamy;

bjork's 1997 record *homogenic*;

the specific youtube video "louise bourgeois peels a tangerine" (thanks lenny!) & also her book *the spider and the tapestries*;

the films of catherine breillat, most especially *barbe bleue, a ma soeur, & une vieille maitresse*;

jericho brown's *the tradition*;

the entire illustrious music career of kate bush, but "song of solomon" is cited from 1993's *the red shoes*;

judith butler's *excitable speech* & *giving an account of oneself*;

jos charles' *feeld*;

heather christle's *the crying book*;

alison cobb's *GREEN-WOOD*;

annie dillard's *pilgrim at tinker creek*;

james elkin's *pictures & tears*;

t fleischmann's *syzygy, beauty & time is the thing a body moves through*;

the paintings of artemisia gentileschi;

pj harvey's 1993 record *rid of me* & her 1995 follow-up *to bring you my love*;

bell hooks' *all about love*;

the collected poems of ted hughes;

elaine kahn's *romance, or the end*;

bhanu kapil's *humanimal: a project for future children*;

bright star: letters of john keats to fanny brawne;

julia kristeva's *powers of horror* & *black sun*;

doris lessing's *the golden notebook,* which i've read a thousand thousand times;

emmanuel levinas' *humanism of the other*;

carmen maria machado's *in the dream house*;

diane middlebrook's astonishing biographies of both sylvia plath (*her husband*) & anne sexton;

joni mitchell's *blue*;

the complete poems of marianne moore;

david naimon's podcast *between the covers*, in particular, his jun 1 2020 interview w nikky finney;

the paintings of emilia olsen, to whom i owe this book's jacket design;

the tv movie *perfect body* (1997);

the *collected poems of, unabridged journals of,* & both beautifully compiled volumes of *the letters of sylvia plath*;

claudia rankine's *citizen* & *don't let me be lonely*;

kate russell's *my dark vanessa*;

may sarton's *journal of a solitude, plant dreaming deep, & recovering*;

eve sedgwick's *a dialogue on love* & *touching feeling*;

the complete poems of anne sexton;

leslie marmon silko's *almanac of the dead,* a book never far from my grasp;

layli long soldier's *whereas*;

susan sontag's *against interpretation & other essays & reborn: journals & notebooks 1947–1963*;

krista tippett's podcast *on being,* a source of great light;

darcie wilder's *literally show me a healthy person*;

the complete works, letters, & journals of virginia woolf;

c.d. wright's entire body of work! my god, what a loss; & what wonder she brought;

kate zambreno's *appendix project, heroines, screen tests,* & her newest "novel," *drifts,* an especially beloved quarantine read;

& rachel zucker's podcast *commonplace,* in which series i have again & again discovered invaluable conversations w poets & other writers which have opened the craft further for me. my endless gratitude to these works & artists, all.

ACKNOWLEDGEMENTS

first, ofc, for my mother, my sister, & my olive—the rocks of my life;

for friends who have uplifted me throughout—

harron—i love our cis journey together; steph—for not killing me; char-lotte & the kitties—what light u bring to the world; rax—my tacky sister-in-arms; nick—for the comfort of ur voice; karen—for saving me when i was at my lowest; rachel—we've been in it for a long while now, & to our too muchness; also, mark, rachelle, emily & grace, emilia, jesse, jazzy, j lamar, amber, elise, yaari, fran, reid, lucy, noot, soren, camonghne, nicky & hunter, greg, kylah, eric & mike, & god, so many countless others; i feel fucking blessed, uplifted, & honored to have a treasure of intimacies in this life! u all have kept me here;

for nancy gray, my best mentor, wherever u are;

for the fucking groupchat! i love y'all! u make me laugh, u inspire me, u keep me tapped in to the world in healthier ways than i am capable of by my lonesome;

for the twitter fam—what luck to feel so adored;

for brendan joyce & kevin latimer, for *GRIEVELAND* & for taking this chance;

for ayla, my other chance-taker;

& for my kevin, my love, excited for this passage...

Also from

JAMIE HOOD

From a rising literary star and the author of
how to be a good girl comes a brilliant, biting,
and beautifully wrought memoir of trauma and the
cost of survival.

Learn more at knopfdoubleday.com